Made in United States
North Haven, CT
15 November 2022

26773908R10067